HORN

by Schulz

PEANUTS © United Feature Syndicate, Inc.

HOW TO USE THE CD ACCOMPANIMENT:
THE CD IS PLAYABLE ON ANY CD PLAYER, AND IS ALSO
ENHANCED SO MAC AND PC USERS CAN ADJUST THE
RECORDING TO ANY TEMPO WITHOUT CHANGING THE PITCH!

A MELODY CUE APPEARS ON THE RIGHT CHANNEL ONLY. IF YOUR
CD PLAYER HAS A BALANCE ADJUSTMENT, YOU CAN ADJUST THE
VOLUME OF THE MELODY BY TURNING DOWN THE RIGHT CHANNEL.

Visit Peanuts® on the internet at
www.snoopy.com

ISBN 978-1-4234-8691-6

HAL•LEONARD®
CORPORATION
7777 W. BLUEMOUND RD. P.O. BOX 13819 MILWAUKEE, WI 53213

Visit Hal Leonard Online at
www.halleonard.com

◆1 BLUE CHARLIE BROWN

Horn

By VINCE GUARALDI

❷ CHARLIE BROWN THEME

Horn

By VINCE GUARALDI

❸ CHARLIE'S BLUES

Horn

By VINCE GUARALDI

◆ CHRISTMAS TIME IS HERE

Horn

Words by LEE MENDELSON
Music by VINCE GUARALDI

◆5 CHRISTMAS IS COMING

Horn

By VINCE GUARALDI

◆ THE GREAT PUMPKIN WALTZ

Horn

By VINCE GUARALDI

small notes optional

◆ JOE COOL

Horn

By VINCE GUARALDI

◆8 LINUS AND LUCY

Horn

By VINCE GUARALDI

With energy

Piano

◆⑨ JUST LIKE ME

HORN

Lyrics by LEE MENDELSON
Music by DAVID BENOIT

◆ 10 MY LITTLE DRUM

Horn

By VINCE GUARALDI

O TANNENBAUM

HORN

Traditional
Arranged by VINCE GUARALDI

🔶12 OH, GOOD GRIEF

Horn

By VINCE GUARALDI

◆13 SKATING

By VINCE GUARALDI

HORN

◆14 RED BARON

Horn

By VINCE GUARALDI

WHAT CHILD IS THIS

Horn

Traditional
Arranged by VINCE GUARALDI